G000127874

The Definitive Guide to
Organizational Backstabbing

To Elizabeth
may we stay afloat
of the drowning
cess pool, known
as the "office
world".
Always,
Sandie
Ballard

The Definitive Guide to Organizational Backstabbing

by Berl Falbaum

Illustrations by Joseph Brancik

Avonstoke Press

Copyright © 1994 by Berl Falbaum

All rights reserved. No part of this book may be reproduced in any manner without prior written permission of the author, except in the case of brief quotations embodied in critical reviews and articles.

Manufactured in the United States of America

1997   1996   1995   1994   4   3   2   1

Avonstoke Press
6964 Crooks Road, Suite 1
Troy, Michigan 48098

ISBN 1-879094-29-0

Library of Congress Cataloging-in-Publication Data

Falbaum, Berl, 1938-
    The definitive guide to organizational backstabbing / by Berl
Falbaum ; illustrations by Joseph Brancik.
        p.   cm.
    ISBN 1-879094-29-0 : $9.95
    1. Office politics--Wit and humor. 2. Business etiquette--Wit and
humor. 3. Success in business--Wit and humor. I. Title.
HF5386.5.F37   1994
650.1--dc20   93-23562
                                                        CIP

Other books by the author

Just For Fun

The Anchor, Leo & Friends

Do Unto Others Before They Do Unto You*

*In keeping with the wisdom in these pages, we stole the above thought from a (former) friend.

It's not what you know or who you know. It's how effective you are at "doing in" who you know.

Table of Contents

Introduction

The Horatio Alger story did a major disservice. It created the myth that if you work hard, keep your nose clean and live by the highest principles, you can—no, you *will*—make it. The much ballyhooed Dale Carnegie course hypes us into believing we can sell or accomplish anything with a fierce belief in ourselves and a super-positive attitude revolving around principles of fair play.

Schools, parents and religious organizations reinforce these concepts. The public generally accepts them.

Hogwash! The premise that hard, honest work pays off ain't, as the song says, necessarily so. Nice guys do finish last. The odd exception proves the rule. Know why we make a big deal about nice guys finishing first? Because it rarely occurs.

We're happy for the nice guys who succeed. They should be rewarded. As a matter of fact, if we had the power to assure who makes it—nice guys or S.O.B.s—we would vote for the nice guys.

Unfortunately, millions of honest people work very hard but find progress in their respective organizations blocked because they are nice. They don't, can't or won't—for whatever reason—practice office politics. As a result, they are doomed to mediocre careers.

So we'll center our attention here on helping those who want to roll past, and over, their colleagues. Women, now one-half of the work force, should not be angered or dismayed by our use of the pronoun "he." The backstabbing work force remains male-dominated. We use the pronoun "he" because, no matter how unfair, "she" hasn't reached equality yet. We pray for the progress of "she," but must reflect reality. On the other hand, most of the backstabbing advice which follows applies to females as well.

Nor do the rules we discuss apply only to multinational corporations. Every organization no matter how large or small—including hospitals, academia, school systems, athletic teams, religious institutions or homeowner associations—advances its backstabbers. Some slight adjustments in technique might be necessary, but office politics is the game played everywhere. It's a national pastime.

The clergy, academia, and others undoubtedly will be aghast at our advice. But the greater the protest, frankly, the more we believe we're right.

If this book helps one reader earn a promotion, then we have fulfilled our objective. Even if it doesn't help you, here's some free advice: Recoup the cost of the book by putting it on the expense account. "Extracurricular studies" ought to do it.

Who Should Read This Book

We're tempted to say "everyone," but that's a little self-serving. Certainly benefits would accrue to:

● High school and college grads, especially those whose ambition is exceeded only by . . . well, by nothing. This particularly applies to those who hero-worshiped Brutus in *Julius Caesar*.

● Anyone in the work force under 40 who may still be foaming at the mouth with ambition.

● Those over 40 who want to know why they did not make it and are curious about what went wrong. True, not much can be done about a spilled career at this point, but maybe you can counsel a son, daughter or friend.

● Those who did make it and attribute their success to talent.

● Those who made it, know why and would enjoy a private chuckle.

Careers Best Served by the Guide

Here is a list, offered in no particular order:

Law	Politics
Medicine	Religion*
Industry	Wall Street
Photography	Banking
Ornithology	Engineering
Academia	Commercial Art
Entertainment	Labor Relations
Sports	Zoology
Law Enforcement	

We believe you get the picture.

*The presence of religion on this partial list may surprise a few naive readers. We don't mean to offend any sensibilities (not really true), but you don't think that some rabbi-priest-minister is assigned to the North Pole because he didn't pray hard enough, do you? Think about it. They all pray. So what separates those who work up the heavenly ladder from those who remain at the bottom? Read on.

Role Models Who Deserve a Word of Acknowledgement

We don't want to sound trite but there really are so, so many people to thank for making this book possible that space does not allow anything approaching a comprehensive list. Each day another inspiration pops up in the press. Here are just a few that stand out from several decades of learning by example:

● Roberto C. Goizueta, chairman of Coca Cola, who received an $86-million, one-year pay and bonus package in 1992 (no, $86 million is not a typo). In his own defense, Goizueta stated that under company provisions this haul could have been double. Chutzpa has been redefined.

● John DeLorean, who made millions and, when indicted, pleaded publicly for contributions to his defense fund. Maybe he and Goizueta talked.

● Ivan Boesky and Mike Milken of insider trading fame.

● William Aramony, the former United Way of America chairman, who received huge salaries and fringes before resigning under pressure from those who don't understand the game. His slogan: "Take Once From All."

● William M. Agee, former chairman of Bendix Corporation, who created the golden parachute. Wear one and the more you goof up, the more you get paid.

● Mary Cunningham, who floated down with Agee—and with substantial rewards for helping lose Bendix to Allied Corporation.

● Sen. Joseph Biden, who ran for president but encountered one little problem: He was delivering other people's speeches. Sometimes that's called plagiarism. When caught, he replied: "I regret I have but one candidacy to give to my country."

● Leona Helmsley, the hotel baroness, who went to jail for tax evasion after proudly proclaiming that "only little people pay taxes."

● Executives who are paid millions in long-term contracts after being fired. Proxies refer to them as "consultants." Translated (for the uninitiated) that means "stay away, keep your mouth shut and you'll get paid for many years." Not being stupid, they do exactly as told and count their money.

● Joe Niekro, the major league pitcher, who was caught by umpires illegally roughing up the ball with a nail file. As umpires approached to question Niekro, he faced the embarrassment of the file falling out of his pocket as millions watched on TV. Of course, viewers were treated to a series of instant replays, capturing the file's descent from various angles. If we remember right, Niekro received a 33-minute suspension and a $2.75 fine, as well as his own copy of the videotape, which he enjoyed playing at parties.

A generic thank you to: academicians who fake their resumes and plagiarize doctoral papers; musicians who lip-synch lyrics; athletes who use performance-enhancing drugs, and politicians who use slush funds for personal expenses—as well as generally misappropriating public monies.

Our special "gratitude" Oscar goes to Rosie Ruiz, who won the Boston Marathon a few years ago—or so it seemed. It turned out that half way through the race, she took a bus to the finish line. Our hat goes off to her. We like to applaud that special touch of class. We savor the vision of her asking the driver how close he stops to the finish line. Ms. Ruiz might have been asked to contribute to this volume, had the judges, sticklers for detail, not pushed her off the victory podium. (See Addendum to Acknowledgements.)

No one, of course, deserves as many thanks as the countless politicians and public figures whose efforts on behalf of backstabbing are chronicled daily in the media. Their help has been invaluable. Thank you, thank you, thank you.

We hope that any deserving backstabbers not mentioned in these acknowledgements will not feel slighted.

Addendum to Acknowledgements

We offer this addendum because we don't want to leave the impression that we admire those who made this book possible. We don't.

Why? If you can't guess, you really need to read this book. We don't admire them for one reason only—they got caught.

Stupido, stupido, stupido . . .

Backstabbers are supposed to do exactly what these luminaries did. But proficient backstabbers never become Page One news. The really good ones retire with millions. They are not held accountable for their tactics. Artists in this field recognize that escaping responsibility is the key to success. They, of course, realize that but we want to make sure you do. Emulate them but keep it private.

So join us in thanking the notorious backstabbers cited above for making this textbook possible. But remember they ultimately failed by being caught and caught so quickly and

unexpectedly they had no time to blame someone else.

Those who want respect in this tome must
exercise their skills with discretion, and a certain *savoir faire* that leaves no one—except your
victims—fully aware of your skills.

With that caveat, read on . . .

1. Principles

" **A** bandon all principles ye who enter here."

That is the principle that should be emblazoned in the minds of all those who seek success.

Cynicism? No. Realism.

Protest as loud as you wish. "I'm going to hold true. I will not compromise. I do have my ethics."

Fine. But be prepared to dwell forever in the house of lower management.

If you're aiming higher—toward the top, for instance—then the fractured Dante in the first paragraph should be taken to heart.

What should be your fundamental truth, your touchstone of success, your unerring compass in your trek to the top?

The Bottom Line. The organization's and, particularly, your own.

Repeat these words: "The Bottom Line, the Bottom Line. Nothing will get in the way of my service to My Bottom Line."

When you believe that, and become totally

1

committed to fulfilling this dictum at all costs, then you are prime executive material.

How will you know when your transformation is complete?

There are several signs. One morning, you'll wake up and say something that makes your spouse do a double take. Some examples:

- "I'm gonna get that sonofabitch because he cost me a hundred grand. Yeah, he was right. He didn't do anything wrong. But do you know what it will *cost* me?"
- "Damn government EPA requirements are driving me nuts. What's wrong with a little pollution in the river? No one ever eats those fish anyway."
- "If we could dilute that concrete just a tad I'd save $50,000."

When you hear yourself saying things like that, you're on your way.

There are other signs. You're "in," or at least making progress, if your gut instincts lead to action that provokes congratulations from the boss along the lines of:

- "Good job, kid. No one will ever know."
- "Cutting those corners saved us a bundle. I'm gonna tell J.B. so you get the credit." (The part about telling J.B. is a lie, of course. We'll discuss the topic of trust later in this book.)
- "That's what I like to see. A little ingenuity." (This one is subtle; but we all know that the "ingenuity" did not involve charitable contributions.)

Nasty, huh? No one ever said it would be

2

easy. If you're feeling uncomfortable with the lesson plan, now's the time to drop out and join the nice guy at some youth award dinner as he tells all the youngsters how "good hard work and a little sweat is the path to success."

❑ *At 5 p.m. don't forget that you are never to go home on time. Never, never, never.*

2. Working Hours

Many rules govern working hours, and some may seem contradictory. The main thing is to remain flexible enough to employ whatever ruthlessness or trickery will produce the best results.

Conventional wisdom dictates you work from 9 to 5. Ignore that. If you are ambitious, the first thing to do is to kiss the spouse and kids goodbye. Tell them that just because you'll only see them once in a while doesn't mean you don't love them. That's why executives have family pictures on their desks—as a reminder that they have families.

A typical day goes as follows:

Arrive at work about an hour early. Call the boss's office immediately. Even if you have nothing to talk about, make sure the boss knows you're in ahead of schedule. If there is no answer, leave a written message—making sure you mark the time—asking for a call when he arrives.

Be careful. Make certain you have inspirational, reinforcing words during this first call of the day. Feel your way when the boss returns

5

the call. If he hasn't had coffee yet and hasn't been able to clean off his desk, he won't appreciate being met with a problem. Bosses don't like to walk into their offices only to be assaulted with some crisis or hot idea from an eager-beaver subordinate. At this time of day, just stroke.

At lunchtime order in, if you can. And make sure the boss finds out that you are eating chicken chow mein in the office. You might have a fellow employee complain to the boss about the aroma. Whatever it takes. Invite him to share the spare egg roll. He might decline and invite you out for a three-martini lunch.

At 5 p.m. don't forget that you are never to go home on time. Never, never, never. Even if your work is completed, hang around for at least an hour. Again, let the boss know. You can call him on a pretext, or walk down to his office to leave a memo. When he spots you, rejoin: "Gee, I didn't know you were still here. Thought you might want this first thing in the morning."

Then, go back to your office and station yourself strategically so you can see the boss leave. Be wary. Smart bosses may come back to check on you. Wait another 15 minutes. Then, if you see the boss returning as you drive away, pick up a Big Mac, return to the office and tell him you went out to buy a sandwich "because it's going to be a long night."

Even if you insist on adhering to 9-to-5 hours, never join a car pool. Car poolers send some very bad signals to the boss. They can never

stay late. They don't *want* to stay late. They associate with gossipy riffraff. In short, car pooling might stave off an oil crisis, but it's simply not the right attitude for someone with career aspirations.

Go in to work almost every weekend, of course, particularly if the boss may be there. But even more points can be earned on weekends when the boss isn't on hand. The key is making sure that the boss finds out you worked on the weekend when he wasn't even there to be impressed. Talk to the guard (who will talk to the boss). Or leave a properly dated message.

We're confident you can find a way.

Here is the best part. Done right, you might not even have to work. If there is a sign-in sheet, register, stay about 15 minutes and go home.

7

But when you sign out, indicate you worked a full eight-hour day. Make sure your name is in the proper position on the sign-in sheet—somewhere at the top. And make sure you know the boss will *not* be visiting the office. Very devilish and dangerous, but one of the few ways of getting points in absentia.

When "working late" don't forget to call your wife. Tell her you're in conference. No calls, please.

At that point, the choice is yours: Stay at work and catch up on a few things, or go across the street and join the boys.

❏ *We never said success was cheap or painless.*

3. Dress Code

If it's true what they say about first impressions—and it is—then dress becomes imperative in one's career.

The boss reads your wardrobe like a good trail guide reads footprints in the sand. The boss receives messages from what you wear, so beware.

Flamboyance, for instance, tells the boss you can't be trusted. It sends a message of nonconformity—probably the most dangerous signal to any organization.

But ultraconservatism suggests you're not a risk-taker. That's just as bad because it also smacks of "extremism" and extremism in organizations is like, well, having leprosy.

Clinging to the middle road, conforming to the accepted dress code, is just as bad. Utter conformity implies—no, screams out—that you are no different than anyone else on the staff.

What's left, you ask? Plenty.

The art is to dress somewhere between the boss and your colleagues. Try to imitate (flatter) him—don't outdo him—but dress better than your

9

staff or equals. Contrary to some nice-guy theories, clothes do make the man—or at least the perception of the man. The right clothes, a notch above the horde without smacking of flamboyance, can conceal a lack of substance beneath. This truism is repeated time and again. The good dresser goes far beyond the gray masses.

Dress strategy may take some serious research, particularly if you're not into clothes. So invite your wife—if she's into the ambition kick—to the office. Introduce her to everyone. Her secret charge, of course, is to check office dress—check labels, shoes, shirts, ties, skirts, dresses.

Strategize with your expert. Set aside about $5,000. Consider it an investment. Check with your accountant on tax deductibility. Then indulge in a shopping spree.

Begin wearing the clothes to the office. Don't wear all the new clothes day after day. That will arouse suspicion. Incorporate your power wardrobe slowly. Don't worry, it *will* be noticed.

Progress will be evident when the boss compliments you on the "nice suit" (or dress). That's success.

He will not commend a wardrobe that is much inferior to his own, certainly not one that is equal or better. This is a very fine line you are treading.

After you establish the right formula, invest another $5,000 or so on more of the same outfits. You don't want to fuss with what has worked.

If no compliments are forthcoming, bad news: Get another consultant and start over again.

10

Expensive? Of course. We never said success was cheap or painless.

You can probably recoup the investment you made for any clothes that don't work by selling them to a nice guy. Tell him you've suddenly gained or lost weight. This does two things: (a) saves you money, and (b) neutralizes some competition.

If you fail again, give up. Conclude that if you aren't sufficiently astute to recruit the kind of advisers you need, what kind of top manager would you make anyway?

❏ *A secretary can inflict a greater political wound than anyone else in the office.*

4. Secretaries

Confession first: We're not chauvinistic and certainly don't agree with the status quo but we have to deal with this section based on the fact that most, if not all, secretaries are still women.

We don't condone the workplace reality but the facts require us to talk in terms of a male boss and a female secretary.

Remember that a secretary can choke off a career, or at least inflict a greater political wound, than anyone else in the office.

Consider the boss's secretary: Flatter the hell out of her. Do whatever you have to do. Commend her looks, tell the boss how good she is—and make sure the word gets back to her. Tease her but tease her good naturedly.

Don't—we repeat, *don't*—imply a sexual advance. Not even with a harmless double entendre or playful look. But do make her feel attractive. This one is a prodigiously fine line. Only advanced students should even try to walk it.

The boss's secretary wants no involvement with the top dog's subordinates for obvious reasons. She's looking out for her own career and status, and knows better than to dally with underlings. A sexual advance, even unintended, insults her and indicates you believe she would cross class lines. So stay at arms length and politicize her with compliments and positive feedback through the boss.

Don't complain if she doesn't forward a messages or forgets to distribute an important memo. Let her know you are aware of the screwup and are *not* bent out of joint. Swallow hard, smile, and collect important points. Respond along the lines: "It happens to all of us, ha, ha."

Your own secretary is another story, particularly in the way the boss views your relationship with her.

If she's a sharp looker, let him know—only by implication—that you may be fooling around with her. *Don't, by God, admit it.* That would create a problem for him from an institutional standpoint. He'd have to take action. But in conversation, with eye contact and body language, admit to a special chemistry.

This is an incredibly complex and subtle piece of deviousness. It indicates you are "one of the boys" and also makes you vulnerable—an important achievement. Your boss has something "on you." A boss likes nothing more than to think he has a vulnerable subordinate.

When the boss visits your office, order coffee or send your secretary on menial tasks simply to reassure him that, whatever the relationship, you are in control. If she's a looker, he'll enjoy it when she smiles and leans over to hand him his coffee. Rough? Manipulative? Chauvinistic?

Of course. But remember, we're talking about getting ahead.

Careful, successful attention to these strategies will give you the best of all worlds—except, of course, your secretary.

Admittedly this is part of the Old Boys Network. But we see signs of a Girls Network being developed. For the time being, we recommend that secretaries read our work, *Getting Even*.

❏ *The key is what you think the boss is doing. Is he a big fudger or a little fudger?*

5. Expense Accounts

If you view the expense account simply as an accounting document, you have much to learn. No other document is as politically potent.

If you believe that good politics dictate that you keep the expense account to the minimum, you are truly naive.

The most important thing you must remember is that your boss considers the expense account a status symbol and an opportunity to fudge some extra money. He is padding his expense account as much as fear of discovery and the threat of jail will allow.

If your own expense account is not padded pro rata to the boss's, someone will notice the difference. Worse, your boss will fear that someone will notice. Expense account padding works down the line. You must pad yours to make the boss look good; your subordinates must do the same because they know you are inflating yours. Thus, everyone cheats and no one squeals because everyone is guilty.

Too cynical? Think for a moment. Do you recall occasions when your boss asked: "Is this all you spent?" Sure you do. You thought the boss was being a nice guy by giving you a few extra bucks. No way. Nice doesn't make it to the top. The boss needed a cover.

No one loses. And it's painless, like cheating insurance companies.

What's more, padding expenses is another sin that can be written off to "everyone does it." So, besides a few bucks, you pick up a few points for avoiding blue-nose morality.

Furthermore, this is non-taxable income, and it always feels good to cheat the IRS.

How *much* does one cheat on an expense account? The key is what you think the boss is doing. Is he a big fudger or a little fudger? And how much of a fudger do you think your subordinates think you are?

Once you have those answers, it's easy. But don't, under any circumstances, outdo your boss. If you figure the boss pads by 30 percent, then pad your account by 25 percent.

What if you have no idea how much the boss cheats? You must take some risks. A good rule of thumb is to use cost plus 15 percent—just like prudent tipping.

That's about average. Don't be too greedy. It's better to make out several expense accounts than to cheat too heavily on one.

By all means, be creative. Remember, the nice guys fill out impeccable expense accounts totally lacking flair. They'll go to a convention in Atlantic City and eat at McDonald's.

No class, no class, and their expense reports are dullsville for the boss.

What if you cross the prudent line and the boss returns one of your expense sheets as unacceptably extravagant?

Sorry, you goofed. You're on your own. Remember, we warned you about getting caught.

❏ *Let others test the water and then take credit when success seems imminent.*

6. New Ideas

Among the most feared and dreaded developments in any bureaucracy is the new idea. So from the outset, forget about making suggestions or proposing new programs. Nothing will cut a budding career off faster than indications that you are an innovator.

This fact is particularly difficult for college graduates to accept. Filled with idealism, hope and promise, they are chompin' at the bit to save the world—or at least to oil some squeaky hinges. Well, young friends, you can ignore our advice and return to school for graduate studies, or you can accept the backstabbing gospel and take the first difficult step up the career ladder of success.

Understand, organizations despise boat rockers. A new idea threatens everyone:

● The boss who did not think of it.

● Other staffers who, by implication, are at fault for not proposing the new idea earlier.

● The accounting department, which already has tidily balanced its version of reality.

● The legal department, which is suspicious of everything.

In short, the entire bureaucracy loathes a new idea. But it respects those who purloin them, make them non-threatening and turn them into something that makes money without rocking the boat.

Your strategy should be to let others test the water and then take credit when success seems imminent.

So, sit back. As you see a new idea working its way toward acceptance, begin dropping hints that you were the one who proposed it at a meeting which none of your listeners attended. You might even backdate supportive memos and file them.

Don't openly accuse the innovator of stealing your idea. Instead, give him credit for "pursuing it."

This is tricky business, no doubt. But properly done, expertly connived, it works wonders for a career. At no point did the boss regard you as a boat-rocker; you did not risk rejection; you got credit for a *good* idea.

Rather than being chastised for "backstabbing" (which is what you did), you got credit for "good politics and judgment." The secret is stealth and invisibility as you co-opt the nice guy's idea.

In some instances, you can work it so that the true innovator—the nice guy—does get some credit, but the boss learns it was you who saw the merit of the nice guy's idea and by adding a

touch of aggression and realism made it fly. The boss will see you as a mover and shaker, and a possible maker of men, who in turn will make him look good.

The nice guy finishes far back in the pack. You earn credit for someone else's work and simultaneously "do in" a competitor.

What more can you ask for?

7. Inviting the Boss to Dinner

It's an ancient tradition, but inviting the boss to your home for dinner is subject to uncontrollable risks. It's poor strategy of questionable effectiveness. This is true whether the boss is male or female.

Male boss: Just asking a male boss to dinner at your home might upset him. He is allowed only so many nights away, and you might be inviting him on the very night he planned to cheat on his wife.

Further, consider the risks at the dinner itself:

● Kids may stomp on his feet, make fun of his hairline, or ask if he works for their father.

● Your wife might say something politically damaging, like: "Fred is always working late at night." The possibilities are endless.

● Your boss might detest your wife's best recipe.

● He might hate dogs.

● He might wonder why you don't have a dog.

● The neighborhood kids might slash his tires.

The point is, such invitations are dangerous. And, as in all political strategy, a key objective is to minimize risk.

If the boss is female and is a feminist, she will resent the whole idea of the "little woman" making dinner to help her husband. If she is married, her husband will be very upset because in a few weeks his wife will be playing hostess to his boss. In a nutshell, it's a no-win situation.

Conclusion: Dinners at home for bosses are counter-productive.

Alternatives: If your boss is male, take him to a topless bar, buy him a drink and even fix him up for the night. Compromise him and he's yours.

Female boss: Take her to a male strip joint, fix her up and she's yours—figuratively speaking.

❑ *Management will be happy to accept your loyalty, but you'll be pegged as a sap.*

8. Loyalty

When you are part of an organization, how loyal should you be? We suggest this formula: Be as loyal as your employer is to you.

So much for loyalty. Get the picture? You can erase the word from your vocabulary.

No one is loyal at the top, though the top demands loyalty from the bottom. Respond, and it will be at the expense of your own career.

Loyalty implies all sorts of things. Cutting costs. Self-sacrifice—a concept considered sacrilege at top management levels. Acting in the exclusive interest of the institution.

When the boss asks for something "out of loyalty," watch out. It means he's going to assign to you some unpleasant task inherited from *his* boss.

Why not succumb to the loyalty call? Because there is little political mileage in it. Management will be happy to accept your loyalty, but you'll be pegged as a sap.

How do you refuse?

That takes some training and expertise, but consider responding along the following line:

"You know, (your boss's name), no one is more loyal." (He knows that's a lie but he also knows he'd say the same thing.) "And I'd like to help." (Another good lie he can identify with.)

"But," (careful now), "I'm not sure if I did this it would be in your interests or that of the department."

Now, that you've set him up, he'll be prepared to accept almost any reason, no matter how ridiculous. The boss just doesn't want to risk his own career. Go ahead and cite a reason out of *Alice in Wonderland.* He'll probably buy it.

Then close with: "However, if you still want me to do this, I will."

You can't imagine how effective that is. The onus is on him. You're indicating that despite the threat to his career—which you have pointed out—you are still willing to go ahead if *he* makes the decision.

Now sit back and watch him squirm. After a few seconds of silence, you'll hear: "I appreciate your candor." (He doesn't.) "And your point is well taken. Let me think about this for a day or so. Don't do anything until I let you know."

Don't even put the item on your follow-up list. It's history. You'll never hear another word about it.

And score a major victory in your career column.

9. Fraternizing

The adage that the world judges you by the company you keep is especially true in organizations—any organization.

The Hindu caste system is liberal compared to institutional cultures. Don't even inadvertently cross "class" lines.

Be forewarned. Maintain the proper contacts but don't cross the line. Otherwise, you will also become an untouchable on the organization chart.

When the boss is around, for instance, never socialize with those below your rank. That includes secretaries, waitresses, clerks or anyone considered "below" you. Let the nice guy go the camaraderie route. He'll talk to the troops in the foxholes. That's fine. It helps you.

The nice guy keeps the troops happy when they grumble about the boss or some policy. The nice guy is the loyal employee who says, "Oh, they must have a reason for that." Or, "Don't worry, they'll take care of us."

If invited to lower-rank parties, don't even acknowledge the invitations. Leave greetings unanswered. One mistake and word will spread through the organization that you "don't quite have it to be part of the upper club."

Equally important, don't socialize with the boss's bosses—at least when he's not present. That would seriously threaten him and your relationship. If the boss hears you attended a function at which only his superiors were in attendance, you can anticipate a demotion within weeks.

The best policy is to attend functions sanctioned or hosted by your immediate superior. He can keep an eye on you at these events. Best of all, you can do significant damage to his career without him knowing it.

The trick (if your boss is the host) is to work the corners of the room with his superiors and complain that the food is cold, or suggest that the drinks are watered down.

All this must be done discreetly. From a distance, occasionally smile at your host, lifting a glass to toast him while inflicting political wounds behind his back.

This is extremely effective because, in many instances, the upper echelon won't remember which minions they talked to at the party. You won't necessarily be blamed for the gossip. Even if faced with such charges arising from the party, feel free to deny them. Alcohol does wonders to the memory. No one could confidently testify that you were guilty.

Alcohol is a wonderful ally in political infighting.

10. Spouses

Like secretaries, spouses can be among the most important political considerations in one's career.

The boss's wife, for sure is the "king" or "queen" maker—and perhaps your own spouse—can make you or break you.

A word about the boss's spouse. Your job is to impress; and, again, we'll assume in most cases it is a woman. (As liberal as the new world may be, if you're a man and your spouse is not a woman, you're in trouble in most of the organizational world.)

You can impress her in several ways. Pay lots of attention to her at social and business functions. Even at the risk of offending the boss, center on his wife. If you spend more time with her than him, he may be happy for the free time.

The ladder-climber must at times be bold. So, sometime during the evening, either with a look or a touch, make a sexual overture. Yup, you read it right.

Be not aghast. The point—usually, at least—is not conquest, but flattery. It may have been a long time since anyone has made such suggestions. She will not forget.

But, you respond, she'll tell her husband. If she does, not to fret. Indirectly, you have complimented his good taste in women. So you have nothing to lose and everything to gain. How can a woman possibly say anything bad about a man who wants to go to bed with her, particularly when he presumably is risking his career? Ah, adventure!

And remember, your boss's wife gets to him at his weakest moments. During lovemaking. While watching the Super Bowl. As he comes home after a hard day's work. When confronting him about his relationship with his secretary. If she likes you, she might even demand that you be given a promotion.

Dealing with your own spouse is a little more difficult because basically we are advising you to debase her. We can't give ironclad advice on this because much depends on your wife's personality. Many will rebel as they should.

Regrettable when considered in terms of a career, but, we hate to admit, understandable. Domination, perhaps even divorce, may be required. (The latter course is not yet a status symbol in institutional cultures, though we expect that may change if present trends continue.)

Tell your wife she must be prepared to take all the chauvinistic abuse possible from your superiors. "Sweetheart," "honey" and other forms of endearment should be welcomed. She also should not be offended if totally ignored.

The difficult part comes when the boss makes a pass at her. Your instructions to her, of course, are subject to (a) your (and her) liberal sophistication, and (b) how much your career means to you (or, more accurately, how much your career means to your wife).

If she rejects him, convince her that the boss was just joking. That probably will be easy. The more challenging conversation involved explaining to the boss that you wife didn't really mean it.

Again, very sexist indeed. Wives might consider borrowing our work, *Getting Even,* from secretaries.

❏ *Announce that you are taking the rest of the day off because of "commitments" and . . . leave with a golf bag over one shoulder.*

11. Double Standard

If you are a manager and have any staff, it is very important that you adopt a double standard. By that we mean one for you and one for the troops. What is good for the elite goose is not necessarily good for the proletariat gander.

To explain: In your staff meetings and when you address groups of employees, emphasize egalitarianism.

Tell them:

● We are all in the same boat.

● All of us must work to cut corners and eliminate waste.

● Let's put in a full eight-hour day.

As the meeting is adjourned, announce that you are taking the rest of the day off because of "commitments" and make sure they see you leave with a golf bag over one shoulder. This is your way of saying publicly, "I am top executive material!"

As for cutting waste, buy expensive furniture for the office and have it redecorated regularly. Purchase pricey trifles, like designer letter openers. To be effective, however, these expenditures must be timed so that everyone knows what you are doing. In a perfect world, this would be half an hour after you turned down a 10-cent-an-hour raise for a 55-year-old widow who has been with the company for 20 years. The reason for the denial: "We must trim costs."

But, you ask, what role does the double standard play in a career? The answer should be apparent.

Our assumption is that you are striving to join top management. You must understand that rules thus don't apply to you. You want to be part of the bourgeoisie. The peasants will never understand why you need expensive furniture, so why explain? Indeed, the upper class has no reason to explain.

What's more, since your boss is abiding by a double standard, he wants to see his lieutenant do the same. You don't think he wants to feel like a two-faced hypocrite, do you?

So show your stuff. Spend while you order labor negotiators to seek concessions. Increase your travel allowance while cutting coffee breaks for employees.

At an appropriate point, stand in the hallway overlooking the troops and, like Patton, tell them: "This is awful; but, damn, how I love it."

❑ *Those who give constructive criticism are like suicidal whales heading for the beach.*

12. Feedback

Most managers frequently urge their subordinates to give them "feedback." The more feedback the better, they say, inviting criticism.

"I don't want 'yes' men (sexist remark) around me," they maintain. "I want honest, constructive criticism."

If you believe that, we'll sell you that famous bridge. Don't be taken in. We have yet to find a manager who was criticized by a subordinate and then rewarded him. Those who give constructive criticism are like suicidal whales heading for the beach.

Why would any manager want criticism from a subordinate? To improve the product or service being provided, you respond. Obviously, you have not studied these pages. That's not the major objective for any upwardly mobile individual in any organization. Remember, all wise eyes are on the Bottom Line. The *personal* bottom line.

Your boss has plenty of reasons for not wanting "honest feedback."

- If it's honest, it probably makes him look bad. (That should be enough to dissuade you.)
- He regrets being too dumb to have headed off the "constructive criticism" with effective leadership.
- Others—including his own boss—might find out what a dope he was.
- You will become a threat if his superiors discover who made the "effective recommendations."

So forget about giving the boss critical feedback. Your job is to make him feel content. If we have to explain how, then this book is too sophisticated for you.

However, this does not mean that "critical feedback" has no role. It does, indeed. But it must be offered deviously.

Your job is to make sure the critical feedback gets to the boss's boss with you getting all the credit, and your boss taking all the criticism. Several possibilities exist:

- You blind copy the boss's boss with your critical feedback memo.
- Better yet, your secretary "by mistake" leaves a copy of the memo on the desk of the boss's boss.
- You mention your reservations "inadvertently" at a party.
- You deliver the critical report to the boss's boss when your boss is on vacation, copying your boss, but explaining that in the interest of time you did not want to wait for his return.

The possibilities are limited only by your ingenuity.

The *Definitive Guide's* principle, then, is this: Flatter the hell out of the boss by all means possible. Tell him how brilliant he is. Never give him a discouraging word.

Then stab him in the back.

*❏ Being unsentimental about
long, dedicated service is
a sure indication of
corner-office destiny.*

13. Firing

Dismissing employees separates the boys
from the men. The properly placed pink slip
is an important means of proving you are top
management material.

How you do it and, more important, to whom
you do it, is the strategic imperative. A few help-
ful hints.

● Do not fire anyone who is incompetent.
That's right. Keep a lot of them around. We
repeat: Do not fire anyone who is not suited for
the job. The reasons were amply covered in *The
Peter Principle*, but we'll add a couple of thoughts.
Incompetent employees, above all, make you look
good by comparison. Why fire them? Further,
they do not pose a threat. That frees you to plan
strategy more effectively without having to look
over your shoulder. If a subordinate is too dumb
to make a move on you, it is, well, *comforting.*

● Another employee you don't fire is the loyal,
trustworthy, dependable soul who comes in on
time, does a good job and never complains.
That's the nice guy. He's the bedrock, the foun-
dation you rely on to grease your way to the top.

Like the incompetents, they don't pose a threat. And, of course, you need someone to do the work.

● You do fire those who demonstrate your own characteristics, particularly ambition. If you have been studying these pages, you should be able to identify them easily.

● You also should fire those in middle-management who have a good reputation as hard workers and who everyone believes have been blessed from the top.

Surprise is the key. You want your underlings to understand that "if it happened to Joe, it can happen to me." It keeps the organization in line.

By showing that you have a tough streak—that you'll fire anyone—your superiors will see your potential. Being unsentimental about long, dedicated service is a sure indication of corner-office destiny.

Always explain a firing by saying it was necessary to "get rid of deadwood." And, of course, always express regrets.

You can heighten the surprise element, by the way, by axing employees who have won awards and have received frequent commendations.

Offer these sacrificial lambs generous severance pay—bribes to keep them quiet—and host "resignation" parties for them. Keys to a new car are an added touch in particularly audacious cases.

Be sure to offer appropriate toasts at resignation parties. Don't forget that, since the entire department is in one place, it's a good occasion to identify your next victim.

The shock ought to be of significant magnitude that the employee takes his leave muttering, "Et tu, Brute."

P.S.: A word about hiring, a topic that does not require a separate section. A few lines will suffice.

During interviews, look for weaknesses you can exploit. Nervousness is always a good sign. A display of confidence is a danger signal.

If a job candidate mouths such promises as, "You will always be able to count on me," or "I am true blue," or "I'm a team player"—then you may have a bona fide nice guy to step on. But watch out. This might be another backstabber who protesteth too much.

When checking credentials, ignore professional accomplishments and telltale signs of character. Always seek a good, honest, unsophisticated worker of average *incompetence*. Your managerial skills will be judged in part by how well you recruit such candidates.

You definitely will need to hire a few genuine nice guys to replace those who have left, wised up, or burned out.

You need a constant influx of nice guy new blood.

❑ *There is no room at the top for a guilty conscience.*

14. Trust

You probably believe that in the quest to reach the top you'll need a mentor, a confidant or, more accurately, a co-conspirator. You assume you'll need someone with whom to strategize and, in weak moments, perhaps someone to whom you can confess.

Not so. The following rule is absolute. No exceptions. You might decide to compromise on some of the other advice given in this book. But *never trust anyone*. Never, never, never. Write that message several hundred times: "Never Trust Anyone."

This includes your spouse, mother or other relatives who might work with you (including your son or daughter). Blood is thicker than water, but no one ever compared it to institutional politics. Never trust anyone.

Okay, assume you are prepared to accept this rule but need help. If you do, you are not cut out for the top anyway. So lower your sights. That may be a brutal message, but you might as well know the bad news early in your career.

Ironically, some of our students felt their first

burning need for a confidant only after imple-
menting our advice—and finding it necessary to
rid themselves of attendant guilt.

Well, if you are not going to make it because
you need help formulating strategy, you certainly
won't make it if you suffer from sniveling senti-
mentality. There is no room at the top for a
guilty conscience. We'll go further: There is no
room at the top for a conscience. Seek another

career, or accept life at the bottom.

Go it alone, friend. Trust only yourself. There are many advantages. You get all the credit. No one will squeal on you. No debts are owed. And only you know the rotten deceit you have practiced.

After you've considered these advantages, the concept of "trust" will never again cross your mind.

But the concept of trust proves valuable in one situation: When talking to a subordinate, always conclude instructions or advice with: "Just trust me."

❏ Spread word of your "loss."
Get to your colleagues
before the boss does.
He'll appreciate that.

15. Recreation

Many amateurs lose out here and career advancement screeches to a sudden stop. They simply don't understand that you can climb by taking a fall. Even many ambitious employees who accept most of the help offered in these pages reject reality on the golf course, on the tennis court or at the bridge table.

Machoism takes over. They just can't throw a game, even with the boss.

On the verge of success, they falter upon the incredibly naive belief that the boss really doesn't care who wins. Don't believe it. He cares more than he cares about the next day's sales report.

So, throw the damned game! No matter how obvious. You simply don't understand your superior's ability to believe his superiority.

Do whatever it takes to lose. Don't be misled by any urging to "give it your all," "come on, give me a match," or "hang in there."

Don't do any of these things. Miss putts. Blow backhands. Forget to count trump cards. Fizzle out on the tennis court.

The next day at the office, spread word of your

"loss." Get to your colleagues before the boss does. He'll appreciate that.

When he needles you unmercifully, laugh and shrug and be a graceful—but totally vanquished—loser.

Tell the boss he could have beaten Jimmy Connors. Or Arnold Palmer.

Watch the effect. It is unbelievable.

"I did play well," the boss will agree. "But Palmer? Not really. Well, maybe on that par five . . ."

Political amateurs think the court or course is the one place they can beat the boss. Not really. It's a short-lived victory, and they'll pay the next morning.

The place to get the boss is not on the tennis court, but in the office.

❏ *A warning on jokes: Make sure you aren't laughing at a serious remark.*

16. Brown-Nosing

This subject must be addressed forthrightly. If we did not deal with it, the *Guide* could not be considered definitive on how to succeed at any cost. Brown-nosing is distasteful, but it is important. Do as much of it as possible.

Why brown-nose? We'll answer that with another question: Why not?

Would top management prefer a brown-noser at its beck-and-call, or an efficient employee who is not available for menial tasks? Would an executive like someone to drive him to work, light his cigarettes and shine his shoes? Or would he prefer to do these chores himself?

The answers are obvious. Besides, having someone cater to him impresses people. And there are some sadistic psychological rewards in watching others debase themselves.

We can almost read your mind. This is one career recommendation that goes too far. That's understandable. But believe us, after you have opened the car door for the boss a couple of times, it gets easier. And it's amazing how many

points you can score when it's just you and the boss driving to the airport.

A few weeks into sycophancy and you'll laugh at jokes that aren't funny, salivate like Pavlo's dogs and you'll carry the boss's briefcase without a tinge of self-deprecation. Think of the criticism Jimmy Carter received for carrying his own luggage. It didn't do much for his image, did it?

A warning on jokes: Make sure you aren't laughing at a serious remark. Sometimes this distinction is blurred among amateur brown-nosers. They pay a heavy price.

Ironically, nice guys can be rivals in the brown-nosing game. Niceness and sycophancy do have some overlap at times. But when the chips are down, and the boss asks for an honest opinion, one he doesn't want, or criticism or when he cracks a joke that isn't funny, the nice guys make two mistakes: they give honest opinions or respond with silence to tasteless punch lines.

No matter what we say, if you make a serious run at brown-nosing, you'll cringe at first. To help you overcome the sick feeling in the pit of your stomach you might want to read *My Life with J. Edgar Hoover* or *How to Kissy Up and Feel Good About Yourself:* Subtitled *Do it Blindfolded,* a pair of rarely discussed but useful tomes.

Both are out of print but still available at some discerning stores which deal with books on management success.

By no means are we suggesting that brown-nosing is not a totally despicable practice. It requires serious intestinal fortitude on the part of both brown-noser and brown-nosee. Such is the price of leadership.

In fact, we finish this chapter with the observation: Better you than us.

❏ *If you're called on first—the worst-case scenario—go immediately to double-talk.*

17. Meetings

Much of our advice involves one-on-one situations. But some strategy does not require going face-to-face with the boss.

For instance, meetings—in the broadest sense of the term—require group therapy skills, if you will. Group dynamics are a little different, and executives-to-be would be well-advised to heed the following suggestions.

First, a few questions: Do you worry about what other people think? Do you try to save them embarrassment? Do you work hard at not upstaging them? If you answered "yes" even once, then we're wasting our time.

But if you answered all three questions in the negative, we're pleased to say your potential is limited only by latent guilt. If you have none you are, of course, right on track.

Here are some rules about group sessions:

● Lay back early. Let your colleagues, as well as the boss, play their cards.

● Note the differences between the boss's position and those of your colleagues.

● Make sure you have the last word in the

meeting. This assures that (a) the boss will settle on his final position before you inadvertently disagree with him, and (b) no one will have a chance to call you to task.

● If drawn into the discussion prematurely, change your mind as frequently as necessary, even if you have to contradict yourself. Confusion is not necessarily bad. It's better to change one's mind to agree with the boss than to exit a meeting opposed to him.

● If you're called on first—the worst-case scenario—go immediately to double-talk. Bullshit, in other words. But make it sound sincere and thoughtful. Your nice-guy colleagues will not blow your cover. The boss will never admit he doesn't understand. In fact, he'll probably commend you with "that's a good point"—forcing others to agree.

The boss won't call on you again because he doesn't want to appear ignorant. This frees you of any duty to talk until you want to, the perfect strategic position.

When it's finally your turn to speak—and this is, remember, the very last word at the meeting—you commend the boss, criticize everyone who differed with the boss even slightly, and end with: "Good meeting, (your boss's name)."

You will know the strategy has been effective if the others pick up their materials and exit, calling you, under their breath, a sonofabitch.

❑ *One traditional comment that keeps employees on their toes is to mark projects with "good start."*

18. Promotions

When you're totally convinced that the boss does not consider you a threat, ask for a promotion. Don't approach him until you're sure you have eliminated all doubt in his mind that you are docile and incompetent.

The unindoctrinated believe that the best time to ask for a promotion is when they've been complimented by the boss's boss. A good word from the "big boss," so the theory goes, puts pressure on the little boss to reward an employee. Not so. It works just the opposite. Remember, the boss wants no threats.

When you feel properly positioned, ask for the promotion in a dialogue somewhat along these lines:

"Gee, boss, it's been a long time since I got another stripe. I know I've slipped in a couple of areas," (reminding him of any incompetence), "but I have learned a lot, thanks to your tutelage, and I really believe I deserve a promotion.

"I also know that (big boss's name) has been a little angry at me," (reminding him you're not big boss's boy), "but you know it was one of those things.

"All I'm asking is that you consider it. Oh, incidentally, I've been discussing other career options with the family."

The above is a perfect strategy. You remind him of your incompetence and then warn that he might lose it to another company. No manager wants to lose a no-threat employee.

If the boss responds with "I'll think it over," start spending the extra money. "Thinking it over" means he's worried you might actually quit. He can't afford the risk. If he were inclined to turn you down, he would do so immediately.

If this strategy is clear to you, then you know what to do with your own subordinates.

You can help yourself by leaving a paper trail leading up to a subordinate's promotion request. Make sure your comments on his work support any future decision regarding promotion.

One traditional comment that keeps employees on their toes is to mark projects with "good start." Such a tactic (a) commends them, (b) implies criticism, and (c), best of all, confuses them totally. They don't know whether to leave the project as is, change it slightly or redo it entirely.

At promotion time, you can interpret the "good start" as you see fit.

This phase of the game is, of course, played on the slipperiest turf. That's because the ultimate in managerial excellence, as judged by top executives, is to deny all promotion requests.

This gives life to the phrase "hope springs eternal" for the less fortunate.

❑ *Let us put it bluntly: Your subordinates can't wait for you to travel.*

19. Travel

Most employees enjoy a few days away from the pressures of office and family. Everyone likes a change of pace. That's why incidental job-related travel is considered a perk.

We understand that, and certainly applaud the opportunity to cheat on the expense account. You can pick up a few extra bucks and there is something to say for enjoying a few drinks at your employer's expense.

Your career, however, can be ruined in your absence.

The next time you accept a trip, think how you feel when the boss leaves town. You drool, right? Damage can be inflicted with little risk of the boss finding out.

So accept the fact that your subordinates feel the same way. Let us put it bluntly: They can't wait for you to travel. They want to be rid of you and they—like you—want to minimize strategic risks.

Is there any way to protect yourself?

Yes, but none of the safeguards is absolute. Consider these choices:

● Assign a stool pigeon, someone who will give you feedback on what's happening in the office while you're gone. The drawback is that much depends on trust. We've already explained how we feel about trust.

● Return to the office unexpectedly. This is not a bad tactic, but it cuts your trip short—defeating the whole purpose of traveling in the first place.

● Plant bogus memos which the ambitious employees can pounce upon in an effort to do you in. Such a maneuver, besides giving you some protection while traveling, identifies those you want to fire or keep an eye on. But the work involved in creating such a scheme might negate the benefits of travel. Careful planning is imperative.

So what's the answer? Well, we suggest you don't travel. Many managers don't listen to us on this subject because they like to get away. More often than not, they suffer the consequences.

Remember, you don't need to travel to cheat on the expense account. Or on your spouse, for that matter.

❏ Never answer your own telephone, even if you have nothing else to do.

20. Telephone Messages

As in life, many times it's the little things that count. Anyone aspiring to a successful career should not overlook strategies in leaving messages and receiving phone calls. Many a prospective executive has been tripped up on trivial detail—such as succumbing to impulse and answering his own phone.

Let's first consider receiving calls. Never answer your own telephone, even if you have nothing else to do. It doesn't look good to superiors, who would never think of such a thing themselves. Also, it's demeaning to let a subordinate think you might stoop so low as to pick up the receiver.

If the boss calls, instruct your secretary *always* to say you are in a meeting, but that she'll interrupt. Answer this way: "Sorry, P.T., but I'm in a meeting." Then, with the mouthpiece half uncovered, say to the empty room, "Excuse me, this is P.T. on the line and we have some confidential business to discuss."

Beautiful.

Having boosted the boss's ego, proceed: "Okay, P.T. how can I help you?"

"Nothing important, but could you bring up your copy of today's newspaper?"

"Sure thing."

The main point is to indicate how busy and important you are when the boss calls.

Now, the reverse situation—telephone calls from subordinates.

Never talk to them on their first try to reach you. That's right. Let them wait. If they have tight deadlines and need your sign-off, make them sweat. As a matter of policy, force them to leave messages with your secretary.

If subordinates insist on calling back frequently, you might relent on the third or fourth attempt. Begin with, "What's the crisis?" Nothing works as well as needless intimidation.

Always put the individual on the squawk box to make them feel uncomfortable. Lead him to believe others are listening. Continue to work noisily in your office, indicating the conversation does not require full attention.

Chuckle aloud a few times, misleading the caller to believe those in the room are making fun of him.

Other rules:

● Never dial a telephone. It's a sign of executive weakness.

● When superiors call and you're out, make sure your secretary indicates you are at a more prestigious locale. "I'm sorry, he is with The Man" will do. Then have her send someone into the men's room to tell you of the call.

● If you've left a message with a subordinate, when he calls back indicate you've forgotten about the call. This (a) indicates annoyance, and (b) drives the subordinate utterly bananas wondering what the call was all about.

If, through some slip, a call you tried to avoid is put through, quickly adopt a computer monotone and tell the caller: "At the sound of the tone, leave your name . . ."

❑ Go ahead and blow that project budget if you must. But avoid the typo at all costs.

21. The Typo

Self-confident as you may be, you probably wonder what is the most serious mistake one can make in any industrial, financial, legal, medical or political organization—any organization whatsoever.

Losing millions of dollars, perhaps?

Leaving a scalpel inside a patient?

Misrepresenting a client?

Making a tax-return mistake that gets a client audited?

Botching a key line in a play?

Nope, none of these holds a candle to the ultimate faux pas, which is (this advice alone is worth the price of the book)—the typo!

Yup, the innocent misprint is the cardinal no-no.

Now, there are important reasons why this is true; but we're not going to give them away. That would impede sales of the five-volume work we're preparing on the subject. It may not quite equal Darwin's work, or Freud's, but we're proud of how it's coming.

So be forewarned. No typos. This is particularly

potent advice if the written material goes up the organizational ladder, but a typo that flows downward does significant damage as well.

The terrifying powers of the typo derive from this fact: Everyone can agree that it's a mistake. The entire organization, in fact, rallies around the smallest such error.

Remember when you committed a typo and fellow workers waved your material in the air, calling attention to the mistake. As you walked into the lunchroom, you heard whispers behind your back, as well as some in front of you.

Or do you remember that performance review that began something like this: "Joe, you're OK, but I have in your files two memos from 1973. Each of them, Joe, contains a typo."

Of course the typos were meaningless trivia. That's precisely the point. Organizations can agree on trivia; they can't agree on anything that really counts.

So go ahead and blow that project budget if you must. But avoid the typo at all costs.

By the way, it would be useful to become computer literate enough to plant typo viruses in your competition's PCs. (Be sure to use an anti-virus program in your own PC.)

Frankly, if you master the planting of typos, you may be able to skip some of the other advice in this book. The phenomenon is that powerful.

Remember, no tyops.

Yeah, we know, a typo. Just having a little fun to see if you're alert. You don't think we'd make that mistake or let our computers be susceptible

to sabotage. Our computers are so virus-proof, the Pentagon is working with us to prevent four-year-olds from infiltrating theirs.

No typos. (Proof we were just joking.)

❑ *You are only bound by the limits of your imagination. The system will believe anything.*

22. Gossip-Rumors

Gossip and rumors are strategically invaluable in the pursuit of career success.

Obviously, like any other skill, it takes training to be effective. Thus, we recommend practice, practice, practice.

Start with "small" indictments of your competitors. For instance, here's a good beginning:

"Did you know that (name) is sleeping with (name) and both took about (dollar amount) out of the till."

As we said, start with small stuff and work your way up. And you must be *subtle.* Subtlety is imperative.

For instance, let's assume you hear the following remark about another competitor: "Did you know that (name) received an excellent performance review?"

When you repeat that information in the office, change it slightly—very slightly. Restate it along these lines: "Did you hear that (name) almost got fired during (his/her) performance review?"

Notice the careful change in emphasis?

Never indicate that you are the source of the information. Remember, you always heard it from someone else and, more importantly, you don't believe it. You are just reporting what you heard.

How ludicrous can the gossip/rumors be? You are only bound by the limits of your imagination. The system will believe anything. Believe us. You can't be too outrageous. Trust us (excuse our choice of words).

The more incredible the better. Indeed, when the gossip you started about a competitor comes back to you from another party, it probably has been embellished even more.

Another good trick is to leave "confidential" memos which indict your competitors on your desk for others to read. These memos, complete forgeries of course, are left there by "accident." And they are written in the name of the head of the organization. These bogus indictments enjoy credibility because the snoops that read them think they were not meant for their eyes. By the time you get back to your desk, the entire organization is talking about their contents.

For help in this type of scheme, read the works of the late FBI Director J. Edgar Hoover. He offers a number of other "cute" do-'em-in-right recommendations. He was a master at his craft, we must admit. We are a little envious.

In any case, set some goals. One rumor a day is more than ambitious for the beginner. But once you get the hang of this strategy, you'll roll.

So be patient. It will come. Meanwhile, some of your efforts must be exerted in squelching rumors about yourself. Don't leave your flank unprotected.

23. Scapegoatism

Let's say you are moving along nicely in your career, having done a sufficient amount of brown-nosing and backstabbing.

When you look back, you see many competitors lying fatally wounded in their career paths.

Does the heart good to take inventory every once in a while.

But suddenly you make a mistake that could cost you dearly.

You stop and think: All that work, all that scheming, all that money and now—because of one little mistake—you might lose several years of progress. Worse, you might be permanently stalled on your drive to the top.

What should you do?

One of the first instincts is to admit the mistake. To put it behind you. That is the traditional principled advice given in standard management journals. It states:

"If you make a mistake, be man enough (sexist remark) to admit it. Everyone makes mistakes. So confess and get on with your job. You'll get credit for being contrite."

The first time we read this, we laughed so hard we almost choked. When we recovered, we discovered that our source was not alone in this recommendation. The entire system gives lip service to the principle.

Thus, we know that it is wrong.

Consider: When was the last time you heard a politician—any politician in history—admit a mistake?

When is the last time you heard any executive admit a mistake?

When is the last time you heard a surgeon admit that the incision was too long, or a lawyer admit that his goof sent his client to the slammer, or an accountant confess to costing you thousands with a slip of a calculator button?

The answer, of course, is never.

So, contrary to conventional wisdom, the course to success is this: *Never* admit a mistake.

If not, then what do you do?

First (after strong denials), work smart, hard and long to cover up the error. Remember that the experts never get caught. Go ahead and emulate Richard Nixon but, by all means, burn the tapes.

Next, launch an investigation. Organizations love investigations. They imply a massive look-see; but when properly delayed, results are never forthcoming. Which is, of course, exactly the kind of result that organizations love to see.

Third, find a scapegoat.

This is extremely important. In fact, we recommend that whenever you start a new job, you immediately begin a file containing names of possible scapegoats you might use in case of mistakes.

Potential scapegoats should be meek, conscientious workers; not particularly likeable; loners.

Remember, scapegoat candidates need not have been involved in the project that went awry. Involvement has nothing to do with fault, organizationally speaking. What organizations want is someone—guilty or not—to blame.

After finding the appropriate scapegoat, do what is necessary to make the charge stick. Plant evidence. Pre-date memos. Post-date memos. Change study results.

Use every dirty trick in the book (re-read the *Definitive Guide* when a crisis approaches). No time to be tentative.

Your reward will come when the boss calls you in and says something like: "Well, I suppose you heard that Joe Conway in Planning was responsible for that screwup the other day."

While feigning ignorance, while denigrating poor Conway for his transgression (but discreetly conveying just a hint of sympathy, because otherwise old Joe was a good guy), count your blessings. Squelch the urge to laugh.

"No, I had not heard," you reply. "Seemed like a good guy."

"Yup, it was him. Thank goodness we found the guilty party. I had him transferred. Let's get on with it."

Success! One more thing:

When you get back to your office, replace Conway's name in your scapegoat file. You can only use a candidate for scapegoatism once.

24. Training

Having gotten this far—thus proving you at least suspect we make sense—you may wonder where you can get some personal training. Who, if anyone, will help you develop these skills?

Excellent question. Unfortunately, the answer is you have to learn on your own. Obviously, no one who practices these policies is going to help you do them in. There is no mentoring. If someone offers, we suggest you beware. You are on your own.

What about business schools and universities? Again, an excellent question. You would think that the schools would recognize, after hundreds of years, that they have failed. Consider: Less than one percent of all graduates ever make it, yet these institutions of higher (or lower) learning have never asked themselves why. It hasn't occurred to them that they may be teaching useless, impractical skills.

One professor at, of all places, the Harvard Business School, apparently recognizing the failure of higher education, started a course in lying, or as he called it, "strategic misrepresentation."

Sure enough, when the *Wall Street Journal* wrote a story on him, the school retreated. The dean of the business school grunted, stammered, protested, and denied, but he had not attended the professor's classes. The professor himself was unavailable for comment.

Pioneers always take the heat, some better than others. Someday, nonetheless, this professor will be credited (no pun intended) with being ahead of his time.

(We know you don't believe this story—and that's good because it proves you're learning—but it was really true.)

The prerequisite for the course, by the way, was failing a lie-detector test. (That's not true.)

So, with no help available, as we said, it's up to you to learn. Do we have any advice for self-teaching? You betcha.

Ideally, you'll start young, doing some relatively simple exercises long before you begin a career. For instance, suppose the newsboy comes to collect. Tell him he already has done so. If he insists you're wrong, slam the door. If you open it when he starts to cry, you aren't going to make it in the world we're talking about.

But if you tell him to get the hell away from the house, you're on your way. Indeed, you might even accuse him of intentionally collecting too often. Rub it in good.

Admittedly, this isn't easy the first time. One eventually becomes hardened after a half dozen times or so to the point where the newsboy will voluntarily forgo a week's pay. That's when you try another exercise, a more difficult one.

Emboldened by success, you can practice on the Girl Scout cookies sales tyke. After you've bought the cookies and polished them off, confront your cute little salesperson and tell her they were spoiled, causing serious illness to your family.

Watch her squirm. Don't let up when you see her discomfort. Stare. Don't break the silence. Yup, take the money when she offers a refund.

The newsboy-girl scout examples are good training techniques. We don't want to give away any more because we are also preparing a textbook on this subject, given the number of inquiries we have received on training for a successful career.

Regrettably, no one really provides training in these techniques, but some of the political fringe groups—those that sponsor survival training in the woods—do teach a few skills that may prove indirectly useful for career advancement.

25. Some Solid Examples

Why don't you, we hear you ask, give me some very specific examples?

You're in medicine, or law, or police work—or whatever—and you want to know exactly what you should be doing.

Sorry, we would like to help you but we can't.

Obviously, there are too many fields and too many situations to be specific.

More importantly, the situation should dictate strategy and tactics. We are dealing with generic principles here.

For example, you are close to making the majors in baseball but some other upstart has the edge on you. Let's say we recommend loosening the screws on his spikes. Might work. But if hitting is what's holding you back, it might be a better strategy to warp your foe's bat.

If you're an actress reading for the part of Juliet, for example, we might counsel you to do in your opposition by changing her script from "Romeo, Romeo! Wherefore art thou Romeo?" to "Romeo, you sonofabitch. What are you doing at my balcony this time of night?" And you might add: "Romeo, you want to what?"

If you're a philatelist you might sabotage your competitor's stamp collections by secretly replacing the glue on his stamps with instant contact nonremoveable cement and, in effect, seal his lips forever.

If some medical student is on his way to the dean's list at your expense, for example, we might suggest you re-calibrate his blood-pressure reader, or install a false thump in his stethoscope.

Specifics are best left up to you to tailor to your field and special circumstances.

As you read these hypothetical examples, we know exactly what's on your mind. We know what you want to ask: How about voodoo?

Good question. Excellent question.

But we must admit, we ain't high on that. Nevertheless . . .

Our position is this: What have you got to lose?

All it costs you is the price of a cloth doll along with some pins. So give it a go. Stick to your heart's content. If you see some results, let us know and we'll be more affirmative in our next edition.

Indeed, if you're effective, open up your own consulting company offering voodoo advice exclusively. Offers some potential for franchising.

We are, however, available for consultation.

Call any time (no collect calls accepted, and we have no toll-free number). We charge by the

value of our advice. Admittedly, we aren't cheap; but remember: You get what you pay for and sometimes that's not true especially if you are dealing with people who have read the *Guide*.

So good luck, and don't let your conscience be your guide. In fact, if you have one, just forget everything we've told you.

26. The Common Denominator

Okay, you're coming to the end of this treatise, so let's pause to see how astute you are.

As you read these pages, has it occurred to you that there is a common denominator to success?

If we were to ask you—and we are—what one characteristic you need, what would you say?

Don't just sit there, stupid, what would it be? No, don't turn the page; don't peek.

A hint—it has three letters.

Okay, another hint: The word starts with "e."

Still nothing, huh?

One more hint: It ends in "o."

You got it, huh? Pretty proud of yourself? Big deal—all you had to fill in was one letter.

Yup: EGO!

Ego is what drives all successful individuals in all organizations. Thus, you need two things: (a) an *immense* ego, and (b) the ability to placate other egos.

We have discussed (b) throughout these pages. By now you ought to know how to be a meek subordinate.

Part (a) is more difficult. Frankly, we don't have the answer, difficult as that may be for us to admit.

We don't know if one is born with an immense ego or if one can develop one. We have talked to physicians, psychiatrists and witch doctors on the subject. We even have interviewed pathologists to see if they have found anything in autopsies.

No luck. So it's up to you. You obviously know whether you have an immense ego. If not, we're not sure how to help you develop one—or even if it's possible.

We have studied photos of those who have made it—made it big. These photos are the ultimate testimonials to ego. Think of the millions of dollars spent on photography each year by people at the top of their fields.

Our studies, in fact, reveal a connection between VIP photos and the employment of chauffeurs. The real reason VIPs, movie stars and overpaid athletes have drivers is that they don't want their photographs appearing on cheap, plasticized driver's licenses without touch-ups.

Think about their embarrassment when they

are stopped by a traffic cop. We once witnessed a VIP actually cry—not because of the fine he faced—but because he looked so bad in his picture. The cop, thinking the VIP was remorseful, tore up the ticket. As the officer left, the VIP tore up the license.

Yes, ego is the ultimate common denominator.

If its location within the human body were ever pinpointed, the ego would become the basis of a medical practice even more lucrative than plastic surgery. The "ego transplant" or "ego enhancement" would be the surgery *du jour*.

Think of some superstar in medicine, law or whatever who is convinced that he is losing the ego battle. He thinks nothing of dropping $15,000 for an ego transplant.

His competitor, of course, wants to out-ego his opponent. The egomaniacs would escalate their dueling scalpels. Unlike other medical markets, this one would never be saturated.

So you might consider starting an ego R&D company. If you isolated this "gene,"—if it is a gene—you would be a billionaire and wouldn't have to worry about anything in this book.

Meanwhile, we hope you came by a sufficiently oversized ego naturally (we really do). Remember, most of the work lies in placating other egos while you "ego" your way to the top.

Conclusion

Well, that's it. It's the best advice money can buy.

Will it guarantee success? Of course not! Yesterday's organizational brainstorm is today's faux pas. We simply can't cover all contingencies.

In this rough-and-tumble world, you have to be flexible, quick on your feet. You have to be ready to deny the affidavit you swore to yesterday.

There is no foolproof road to success. This book is a road map, but remember: "Construction is always under way." The key words are: Improvise; strategize; scheme. We think you should grasp the idea by now.

Are there any non-fiction or fiction characters for further study? Indeed! We recommend Shakespeare's Iago. This master of intrigue could do it all but, unfortunately, he made one major mistake. He trusted someone—his wife.

You have already been well warned about trust. (See the chapter on "Trust.") So, if you fall into the same trap, you have no one to blame but yourself. Study Iago thoroughly, particularly the mistakes so you won't repeat them.

Richard Nixon's career is not a bad case study. But he also got caught. We have warned you about getting caught in the Addendum to Acknowledgments. So learn from his ineptitude: As we said, destroy the evidence!

In short, all villains—in literature and in public life—offer valuable lessons in how to succeed at any cost. None, however, had the benefit of the *Definitive Guide*. They made mistakes, or we would not be able to call attention to their valuable example.

How confident are we of our advice? Will we stand behind it?

If you tell anyone you read these strategies here, guess what?

We'll deny it.

Hee, hee, hee . . . Got the picture?

Endorsements

We asked experts in the field for quotes on *The Definitive Guide to Organizational Backstabbing*, and we received quite a few. A few are published below. The reader will understand why all wished to remain anonymous.

"Insightful . . . Falbaum understands the system . . . amazing, since he never really got anywhere."
> —CEO of a Fortune 500 company.

"What Falbaum doesn't deal with is the psychological lift one receives for screwing someone . . . it's a real high . . . but then he never experienced it. Still recommend the book."
> —One who ignored the nonsense of Management Guru Peter Drucker.

"Gave me feelings of deja vu . . ."
> —Millionaire (possibly billionaire) inmate doing 12 months in minimum security for insider trading. (Editor's Note: Not bad when one considers the return on investment on an annualized basis.)

"Wish it had been available 30 years ago."
        —Retiree with traditional gold watch.

"The bastard . . . he gave it all away and for a mere $9.95. Now I understand why he didn't make it."
        —International cartel executive.

About the Author

How did the author learn these lessons? Well, it started when he was a reporter for the *Detroit News*, covering general assignment stories and then becoming chief of its City-County Bureau. That probably offered the best opportunity for backstabbing research. Everyone blabbed to him—off the record, of course. This was an invaluable period.

Then he served in the executive office of Michigan's governor as administrative aide to the lieutenant governor for four years. There he learned that professional politicians aren't half as nasty, at times, as the so-called amateurs.

For the next 15 years, he had a front-row seat in corporate life, learning the lessons of institutional politics. He served in the PR departments of three U.S. corporations as a speechwriter, press spokesperson and investor relations manager. At one company, he made it to VP.

He has taught journalism and PR part-time for 25 years at two of Michigan's state universities, trying desperately to maintain some idealism. He has taught newswriting, constitutional law of the press, and media ethics. His lectures come from other textbooks. He does not use the *Definitive Guide*, particularly for the course in ethics.

Falbaum has done extensive freelance writing and has published two other books, *Just For Fun*, also satire, and *The Anchor, Leo & Friends*, a book about a bar in Detroit which for more than two decades catered to Damon Runyon-type characters, mostly newspaper people, politicians and a gambler or two. Many came in to drown their career sorrows—not having had the *Definitive Guide* to help them along the way.

Falbaum lives with his wife, Phyllis, in West Bloomfield, Michigan. His wife, a fourth grade teacher, refuses to expose her students to the *Guide*, although Falbaum believes that at that young age this book really could make a difference in their futures. They have two daughters, Julie and Amy, who are ignoring the *Guide* in pursuit of their careers. Despite his newest book, Falbaum has no plans to enter full-time career counseling.